Praise f

"This is one _____ _____ _____ highly enough. It is simple, clear and so very much needed! If you are a pastor get it and read it. If you love your pastor, get it, read it, and then serve him well!"

Daniel L. Akin
President
Southeastern Baptist Theological Seminary

"Since few pastors I have known would ever broach the subject of their pay, we all owe a debt of gratitude to Art Rainer for advocating for this subject with such spiritual sensitivity. Paul admonished the Corinthians-and us- writing, "The Lord has commanded that those who preach the gospel should live from the gospel" (1 Cor. 9:14). It is of interest to note the Apostle's divinely inspired choice of words. He says the Lord "commands" this. It is not an option for the church in caring for those ministers who serve with them. Far more of those God called servants in the church I have known over my decades have been underpaid than have been overpaid. Yes, "the laborer is worthy of his wages." Church leaders should read and heed this volume with conviction and compassion."

O. S. Hawkins
President/CEO
GuideStone Financial Resources

"There are some people who are well informed on churches. There are other people who are well informed on finances. But only a few people can really speak well to the topic of church finances. Art Rainer is one of those people. Having worked closely with Art in a local church context, I can confirm the effectiveness of his approach. Indeed he is one of the best. This book may very well be the best overview on church finances you can find anywhere."

Dr. Jimmy Scroggins
Family Church

The Minister's Salary

And Other Challenges in Ministry Finance

Art Rainer

The Ministers Salary
And Other Challenges in Ministry Finance

© 2015 by Art Rainer

Published by Rainer Publishing
www.rainerpublishing.com

ISBN 978-0692364673

Printed in the United States of America

For Sarah

Contents

Foreword

A<small>RT</small> R<small>AINER</small> <small>LOVES THE LOCAL CHURCH.</small>

Of course, you may rightly say there is a bit of prejudice involved. After all, he is my son. And I do confess that I think very highly of him.

But I think I can say without prejudice or familial bias that Art Rainer loves the local church.

I saw him and his wife, Sarah, get involved in a new church in Lexington, Kentucky. I saw his willingness to take on any task that might help the church and her leaders. From there, I saw his passion to serve the bride of Christ in a church in West Palm Beach. He served on the staff at that church and loved the people, loved the pastor, loved the staff, and loved the community.

Now he is in North Carolina, serving as vice president of Southeastern Baptist Theological Seminary. And guess what else he and Sarah are doing? They are serving with enthusiasm in a church. This man really loves the church.

So what is my point in talking about Art's love and passion for the local church? I want you to know that the book you are about to read is framed in a total commitment to local congregations. Art Rainer will broach some tough and sensitive issues, mainly because the issues are related to money. But he will do so in the context of self-giving love for the church.

I read the book from cover to cover. And I must say that I can't ever remember reading such a powerful and succinct discussion of minister's salaries and benefits. Indeed, after I finished reading the book, I started thinking that this book needs to be in the hands of every leader of every church in America. It is just that good.

Here is what Art gets. He gets that a healthy church has a spiritually and emotionally healthy pastor and staff. And he gets that if pastors and staff are distracted and discouraged about money issues, they are not as effective in their servant leadership of the church. Of course, if they are not effective leaders, then the church is not healthy. Art gets that. And such is the reason he shares the issues with passion and heart.

Don't think you will get bogged down in numbers and statistics in this book. While Art provides ample documentation and support for his statements, he presents it in a way that is both fun and inspiring. His real-life case studies, where only the names have been changed for confidentiality, will grabbed both your mind and your heart. You will learn new facts; but, even better, you will be motivated to serve the local church with greater heart.

My guess is that you wouldn't be reading this book if you didn't have love and concern for local congregations. Indeed, I would conjecture that you love your own church very much. And you desire God's best for your church.

When you love the body of Christ in that manner, you desire to care of those who have been called to lead and serve there. That is what Art is ultimately communicating in this book. That is his passion. That is his love.

So get ready for a fascinating journey into the world of church finances and ministers' salaries. Get ready to learn new facts, and perhaps, learn new passions for caring for those who care for the church.

This book needed to be written. And, of course, it needs to be read.

Read it now with a prayerful heart and open eyes.

Then tell someone else they need to read it as well.

It is just that powerful.

And it's just that important.

Thom S. Rainer

Author of *I Am a Church Member* **and** *Autopsy of a Deceased Church*

Chapter 1

**Solving the Mystery
of Ministry Finance**

When I was a small boy, I went with my dad to the *Hands On!* museum in St. Petersburg, Florida. One of the more popular attractions then was "the Black Tunnel." Basically, it was a huge maze where no light could be seen.

My dad, who was holding me tightly at mom's insistence, told me to hold my hand right in front of my face.

With eyes wide open, I could not see my hand. I could not see anything. The difference of view between eyes open and eyes shut was indiscernible. The attraction lived up to its name. Darkness surrounded us.

The only way we could get from the beginning of the maze to the end was to feel the walls and the openings in front of us. You either had to find the exit on your own, or yell to the operator that you wanted out.

An occasional terrified, lost scream let you know that someone was about to choose the latter option.

Many ministers enter the world of ministry finance with that same perspective. You feel like you are in this dark tunnel and don't know how to find the light of the exit. All of the strange rules and regulations make little sense. Tax codes are complicated enough, but they really look messy when they deal with ministers' finances.

Should I opt out of Social Security?

How much housing allowance do I take?

Do I have enough for retirement?

Should I ask for a raise?

Why do I even need to care about my financial picture?

This book was written to shed light on some of the issues that seem to burden ministers the most. Financial issues for ministers can be very confusing. I can relate. Even though my educational background centers around business practices, I found myself with a pretty steep learning curve when I joined a church staff. Finances and tax law were enough of a challenge when I worked in the business world, but it became a real challenge when I became a pastor in a church.

And I was not alone. And neither are you. Conversation after conversation with ministers made me keenly aware that there is a financial weight felt by many ministers.

Caleb was behind on his bills. His marriage was struggling under the stress.

Linda was upside down on her house. Their current house was too small for their growing family, but they could not move.

Mr. Jackson wanted to retire, but did not see how it was feasible. Past normal retirement age, he still worked to cover living expenses.

Don was getting conflicting opinions on whether or not he should opt out of Social Security. He did not want to make a mistake. Fear gripped him.

Though I was a student of ministerial finances myself, I began to help those who were trying to make some sense of their financial picture. And the more I helped, the more stories I heard, and the more burdened I became for these men and women.

The selection of addressed topics in this book was originally derived from weighty discussions with ministers struggling in this area of their lives. These were good people in bad situations.

A recent survey asked those who serve in churches several questions that related to their financial concerns. The results provided the primary questions and concerns of ministers. These results aligned with the conversations that were had with the ministers. And it is these consistently faced issues that are addressed in the upcoming chapters.

Who is This Book Written For?

I include the word "minister" rather generically in this book. Though I'm usually referring to the pastor, I also realize that a number of other people who serve on church staffs and other organizations have an interest in this topic. Indeed most of the information throughout the book is applicable to them as well. And because there are so many different titles for ministry staff, I'll keep it simple by talking about ministers.

I naturally anticipate that many of the readers of this book are ministers serving churches, denominational organizations, parachurch organizations, and other Christian groups. So you are the primary audience. I want to do everything I can to shed light on the strange and confusing world that is often perceived in ministry finance.

This book is also for those people we often called laity or members of the church. Some of you may be serving in positions of influence in the church: lay elders, deacons, finance committee members, and other key positions. The pastorate can be a very isolating position. Often, your pastor will be hesitant to approach you with his financial concerns. You need to know the unique financial issues your pastor and other ministers face. You need to be an ally and an advocate. It is my hope that this book will strengthen your confidence and your ability to stand beside your pastor, specifically when dealing in the financial realm.

What This Book Is

It is my hope that I have approached this book with both simplicity and clarity on key issues. The primary focus is the individual minister. I try to give you enough information to enlighten you without giving you so much detail that it drowns you. It is my desire that this short book is both holistic about finance but not comprehensive to the point of confusion.

The Minister's Salary is not a comprehensive book on tax codes related to the minister or to every financial issue a minister may face. Those books serve a very good purpose. But here is the challenge. Either you need to know all that's in those books, or you need someone else to know that information for you. So do not just toss them aside. In fact, near the end of this book, I'll share with you one of my favorites of the more comprehensive books on ministers' finance.

Where We Are Going

Each of the chapters could be read as separate instruction guides. Indeed, you might choose to jump ahead to a chapter that is of most interest to you. And that is fine. But, not only did I choose the chapters according to your expressed need, there is a reason for their sequence.

In the second chapter you will read something that I've never seen in a ministers' finance book. Many people in your community have access to some aspect of your finances. It can be a scary thought. Your reputation, even your entire ministry, is at risk if you do not handle your finances well. So we will look at why it is important for you to keep your financial reputation above reproach.

In the third chapter, we talk about retirement. You may wonder why I put a chapter about the end of ministry at the beginning. First, I hope a number of younger ministers read this book. I hope they hear clearly why it's important to deal with retirement issues at a young age. I hope that healthy financial habits are initiated earlier in life. When it comes to personal finances, it is necessary to start with the end in mind.

Second, millions of Baby Boomer ministers are retiring every year. Many are shocked to discover how unprepared they are for this era of their lives. I hate telling a pastor that he needs to continue working past normal retirement age to survive. I try to offer some guidance for those either facing or about to face such an awakening.

In chapter 4, I get down to the basics of how much money you make. Is it sufficient? Is it fair? What if you can't pay your bills? Do you have an income problem or an expense problem? And how do all of these issues relate to the biblical qualifications of being a minister?

Two of the bigger mysteries in minsters' finances are the housing allowance and Social Security. In chapter 5, I look at these two issues in some detail, but in simple language. I try to lift the veil of confusion as it were.

In the sixth chapter, I talk about the need for you to have a team to work with you on financial matters. It doesn't have to be a formal team, just a two or three people you trust. Many ministers have a friend in the church, preferably someone knowledgeable about personal finance, and someone to prepare or help prepare your tax returns. I think you'll appreciate the team approach to help you through these sometime murky waters.

Now that you have the outline, let's get started.

Chapter 2

Money and the Minister's Reputation

THE FOLLOWING STORY IS TRUE.

I wish it were not.

Perhaps this particular case is an isolated or extreme case, but I do not think it is. At least parts of it have been repeated too many times with other ministers.

Of course, the names have been changed.

"Tony" was pastor of one of the larger churches in town. Though this town in a Southern state would not be classified as a city, it had a population of 23,000 and offered a number of amenities. It was a little over an hour from a large city, so residents felt like they had the best of both worlds. They enjoyed small town traffic with larger city amenities.

Tony had been at the church about eighteen months when the talk began. The first words of concern came from a local drycleaner. The pastor had six months of unpaid bills and late charges. A member from Tony's church overheard a conversation between the pastor and the local drycleaner. He had asked for Tony's payment on his order. The owner said he could no longer allow Tony to pay on a charge account.

The pastor just smiled and picked up the clothes. "Just put it on my tab," he said. "I'll pay the bill next week."

The next week came and went. No payment was made.

The cable company was less tolerant. They were owned by a national company that had strict rules about bill payments. They had threatened on three different occasions to turn off the television service.

Tony would typically pay the bills a day or two before the turnoff date.

Exacerbating the problem was the pastor's attitude. For example, a number of church members commented how Tony and his wife would ask to join them at the table at a restaurant. When the bill came, Tony made no effort to pay. The church members paid for the entire party, but the pattern began to irritate many people.

By the time Tony's finances moved from problems to meltdown, church members and other community members were abuzz talking about this irresponsible pastor.

Tony had damaged his reputation.

The meltdown became evident when the pastor received notice of foreclosure on his home. He called his local banker, a friend in the church who had helped with the mortgage, to plead for more time. The banker, though, could not help. Tony's mortgage had been bundled and sold. In simple terms, a faceless out-of-town mortgage company now controlled the pastor's financial fate.

The banker offered to help Tony. He spoke bluntly to his pastor. He told him that he needed to see anything and everything related to his finances: bills, checkbook, statements, and notices from creditors.

The banker was astounded at Tony's mess. There were unpaid bills in 14 different businesses in town. Some had cut off the pastor completely. Tony's credit report was in terrible shape. And he obviously had purchased a home where the monthly payment took a huge chunk of his income. The cable company had, by this time, cut off service. Other basic utilities were about to be cut off as well. His five credit cards were at their maximum limit and past due.

The situation was a mess. And most church members knew at least parts of the story, not to mention other community members who knew of the plight as well.

The banker moved quickly. He refinanced Tony's house. He paid off the existing mortgage company and paid all outstanding bills from the new mortgage. It was a risky move. The new mortgage was about ten percent more than the value of the house.

The banker counseled Tony that he had to live frugally. He could not use his credit cards anymore. He had to pay everything on a cash basis for several years. Any deviation from the plan would put Tony back where he was financially. The pastor assured the banker he understood.

Nine months later Tony had accumulated significant new debts and was four months behind on his mortgage payment. The bank foreclosed. Tony declared bankruptcy.

Pastor Tony was fired by the church before he reached his third anniversary there.

Tony's case may sound extreme. And I hope for most of you it is. Unfortunately, a number of ministers have similar stories. And many more can relate to parts of this story.

In this chapter, I want to share with you how ministers typically damage their reputation with financial mismanagement. These are practical, real-life examples that can affect any of us.

Failing to Pay Bills

It does not take long for an unpaid bill to become a part of a minister's reputation. Let me give you a true example. "James" was a pastor in a fairly large city. He paid his bills promptly and he was a good steward of his money. He mailed his electric bill one particular month about two weeks before its due date. Somehow the payment never made it to the electric company.

To this day, James does not know what happened. Did it get lost in the mail? Was it mishandled at the electric company? Was it applied to a wrong account?

A clerk at the electric company was sorting the past due notices when she noticed James' name on one of the notices. Though she broke protocol and could have been fired, she told her good friend about the past due bill that very night. The friend was a member of James' church and smugly mentioned his "mismanagement" to him at church the next day.

James was stunned. He had yet to receive the past due notice, and he knew he paid every bill on time. He looked in his checkbook that afternoon to see if the check had cleared; it had not. He made a special trip to the electric company the next day to see if there was any error. When no one could find any record of his payment at the company, he immediately wrote another check. He also handed them a letter of apology he had prepared earlier. The letter indicated that the check must have been lost, but he still felt burdened to offer the apology.

I felt terrible for James, but he understood the consequences of his testimony, particularly when it is related to financial matters. This pastor did nothing wrong, but through some type of mess-up over which he had no control, his bill did not get paid. As soon as he knew about it, James paid the bill with an apology.

Ministers, this rule is plain and simple: pay your bills. First, it's the right and legal thing to do. Second, you may be surprised to learn who knows about any unpaid bills. Word travels quickly. And, for better or worse, it seems to travel most quickly when the news is about ministers.

Failing to Give Generously to Your Church

Some ministers have this strange idea that no one knows how much they give to the church. Even if the church has a financial secretary who is not a church member, your level of giving will somehow make it to many church members. You cannot expect your members to tithe if you don't tithe. You can't expect your members to give sacrificially if you don't do so.

Another tragic true story took place several years ago. The pastor asked for help doing his tax returns because he had just been fired from his church. He could not afford outside assistance, so I was glad to help.

As the pastor and I chatted about his plight, I felt comfortable asking him to tell me the story about his dismissal. Much to my surprise, he was totally at a loss for the reason. From his perspective, everything was going well. He had been at the church just a little over a year. The church was growing, and the members seemed pleased.

Out of the blue, the elders called a meeting and asked him to be present. They simply told him that they thought it was best for him to leave, so they voted unanimously to dismiss him. He was given a relatively generous six months severance contingent upon his gracious resignation to the church, and departing within three weeks.

Something didn't fit in his story, but the pastor seemed sincere. I really had no reason to doubt the veracity of what he told me.

I then asked for his tax documentation. He got me all that material the next day. Within an hour, I had a good idea what had transpired at the church. The pastor had a salary of $75,000, but he had given only $1,000 to the church the previous year. His total gifts amounted to just slightly over one percent of his income.

When I told him my hypothesis, the pastor was incredulous. He really did not believe that anyone other than the financial secretary would know the amount of his gifts to the church. But he called an elder at the church, a pretty good friend, and asked him the question directly. Had he been fired because of his anemic giving?

The elder did not lie. Yes, he confirmed that was the reason for his dismissal.

You cannot ask church members to tithe if you are not a tither. You cannot ask church members to give sacrificially if you do not give sacrificially.

But you can expect many members to have a good idea what you give to the church. Your integrity and reputation are on the line.

Assuming an Entitlement Mentality

Some pastors and other ministers seem to think that their position gives them the freedom to ask for handouts. Pastor Tony in the previous example was a true story. He and his wife would impose themselves at church members' tables at restaurants to get a free meal.

Other ministers have been known to expect discounts or even freebies from merchants and service providers. Still others "borrow" money from church members with no expectation of ever paying back the loan.

There are also too many stories of ministers currying the favor of more affluent members with hopes of receiving financial handouts and "deals" on purchases. Sure, there will be time when a minister receives a financial gift from a church member. And most times it should be accepted with grace and gratitude. But ministers who seek such favors quickly harm their reputation and ministry.

Entitlement mentality has no place in Christian ministry. It has no place with those who have been called to lead the church.

Understanding Your Credit Score

There is a number out there "in the cloud" that tells the world about your financial reputation. Theoretically, you have to give permission for someone or company to look at it, but it's viewed by many. Don't think for a minute that your number is a secret. Indeed, you may be surprised how many people know about it.

Every time you apply for a loan, it affects your score. Every time you make a payment on a loan or a bill, it affects your score. Every time you fail to make a payment, it affects your score. Every time your credit limit goes up or down, it affects your score. Every time you borrow, it affects your score. And every time you pay down your debt, it affects your score.

Your credit score is a powerful number. It will determine whether you can borrow, how much you can borrow, whether you should be hired for a job, or whether you can purchase certain items.

The credit score number used to be shrouded in mystery, but we know more about it today than ever. And you need to know about your own credit score as well.

There are three large companies that gather most of the credit information. The three large credit bureaus are Experian, TransUnion, and Equifax. There are other smaller credit bureaus, but these three dominate the industry. You are entitled to one free credit report within a 12-month period from each of the credit bureaus. They will give you credit history, but they will not provide the all important credit score for free. Just Google the name of one of the bureaus, and you will be guided on how to get your report and score.

I strongly recommend you pick one of the three credit bureaus each year to get your free credit report. I also recommend you pay the additional fee, usually about $15, to get your credit score with the report.

You will be given a guide to help you understand your score, and how you can improve it.

The credit score may be the single most important part of your financial reputation; that is why I'm taking a few moments of your time to speak to you about it.

So what are the factors that affect your credit score? There are basically five components, but each component is weighted differently.

Factor One: Payment History

Prior to 2009, over one-third on your credit score was based on how promptly you paid your bills. The weighting is not as great today, but it's still very important. Paying your bills on time can mean the difference between an exceptional credit score and an average credit score.

You can have many of your bills paid online by automatic deduction, or you can make the entry yourself. Don't just throw the bill in a stack when it arrives in the mail. Look carefully at the due date. If you are paying the bill by regular mail, make certain you give ample time for mail delivery and posting. That usually means mailing it at least four business days before the bill is due.

In the past, one late bill could really mess up your credit score. Today, the credit score takes into account that someone will be late occasionally; the score is more about a pattern of payments. For example, I recently had a late bill. Now I didn't know I had a late bill until I received notice from my utility company that I was past due. I had never received the bill. I called them immediately and paid my bill over the phone by credit card. I checked my credit score a month later. It had not been negatively impacted by the one late payment.

Still, it is imperative to pay your bills on time. Not only is your credit score at risk; your reputation is as well.

Factor Two: Amounts That Have Been Approved to Borrow but Have Not Been Borrowed

This second factor is a weird one. You get higher credit scores for a larger available lines of credit on your credit card, but your score is lowered if you keep an outstanding balance on your card. It's the same thing for a home equity line of credit. If you have a $10,000 home equity line available, the credit bureaus love you. But if you actually borrow that $10,000 your scores will quickly drop.

Why do credit bureaus have such weird scoring systems? They are very concerned that you will always have available borrowing power. From their perspective, as long as you have the ability to borrow, you can pay your bills. If you max out on all of your credit cards and other lines of credit, however, you have used up your borrowing capacity and your score is lowered.

You need to watch this aspect of your credit carefully. It is more heavily weighted that it was prior to 2009. Some have surmised that, in the "secret formula," which is your credit score, this factor may weigh more heavily than any other.

So, from a credit score perspective, it's better to have a few credit cards with a balance that does not exceed 50 percent of your available credit, and preferably no more than 33 percent. But I cannot advocate having a number of credit cards myself. The more credit cards we have, the greater the temptation will be to use those cards and increase our consumer debt.

That's where many ministers get in trouble. They spend too freely on borrowed funds such as credit cards, and eventually are unable to pay their bills.

Factor Three: Length of Credit History

The credit bureaus like you to keep your same credit cards for a long time. In fact, if you have kept a credit card over seven years, they view it favorably. If you've kept three credit cards for over seven years, they view it even more favorably. Having more than three credit cards does not help your credit score.

Now here is the clincher: your scores improve if you charge a small amount on each card and then pay the balance off each month. I just have trouble advocating that a minister use three different cards every month. The temptation to incur too much consumer debt is too high.

This factor counts around 15 percent of your credit score, so it is wise to have a long-term relationship with a credit card or bank. But don't let the long-term relationship lure you into unwise borrowing habits.

Factor Four: Credit Inquiries and New Debt

When you apply for a loan or a credit card, the lender checks with the credit bureaus to get your credit score. That inquiry lowers your score, at least for a season. And the more the inquiries, the lower your score will be.

Now here is the double whammy. If you decide to borrow money or get the credit card, the new debt will lower your score even more. These factors are not as detrimental to your score as they were prior to 2009, but you still need to avoid applying for numerous credit cards and loans in a short period. Most of the credit bureaus weight this factor at about 10 percent of the total credit score.

But what if you want to apply for four or five loans to buy that new car to see which one will be the best deal? The good news is that all inquiries on an automobile loan within a fourteen-day period are counted as only one inquiry. If you are shopping for a house, all mortgage inquiries within thirty days of each other will be consider only one inquiry as well.

Factor Five: Type of Debt

There are basically two types of debt: installment and revolving. Some people consider mortgage debt to be a third type, but it's basically just a long-term version of installment debt.

Installment debt is borrowing a specific amount and making payments until the loan is paid off. An automobile loan is a good example. A mortgage loan on a house is an example of a very long-term installment debt.

Revolving debt is the ability to borrow up to a certain amount; as long as you are below the limit, you can borrow whenever you want. A credit card is the best example. You may have a $5,000 credit limit. If you owe $4,000 and are making timely payments, you can borrow up to another $1,000. Or if you pay your credit card balance to $3,000, you can borrow up to another $2,000.

In your credit score, installment debt is favored over revolving debt. The credit bureau knows you will not borrow any more on your installment loan. To the contrary you are paying down the balance. But a revolving credit card may have a balance indefinitely, as long as the cardholder is making the minimum payments on time.

It's All about Your Reputation

Your credit score gives you a quick, easy picture of your current financial reputation. Most ministers do not have financial training or backgrounds. And most do not get into financial trouble because they are malicious or greedy.

They simply do not grasp how a credit card with an 18 percent annual percentage rate can increase your debt dramatically.

They don't understand that you can buy a house that costs so much your monthly mortgage payments make you "house poor."

They don't often realize how borrowing for a new car can hurt their financial ability as opposed to paying cash for an older car.

They are good pastors, well-meaning pastors. They love the Bible, and they love their church. But, unfortunately, there are pastors out there with a tremendous understanding of the Bible but not of a balance sheet.

Because of this, we have ministers with no clue that they are moving toward financial problems or ruin unless something changes. Their reputation is on the line, and, sometimes, their ability to do ministry as well.

Money is one of the most pervasive topics in the Bible. The pastor, if he preaches the entire counsel of the Bible, will preach and teach on the subject numerous times in his life. He will encourage church members to be faithful in their financial stewardship. He may even have special times of study of sound and biblical financial management.

And yet, his own financial footing is eroding. Each paycheck seems to have to be stretched further and further. He feels the strain. His family feels the strain. His marriage feels the strain. Whether they recognize or not, his church is experiencing the consequence of the strain.

He finds himself questioning his ability to lead his church. Doubt consumes him.

When it is all said and done, I do hope you learn many of the financial issues facing ministers today. I hope you will come away from this book with the ability to provide better financially both now and in the future.

Indeed, I did not write this book just to be another financial primer. I wrote this book so that ministers could become better managers of their finances and their households. This book also gives church members a glimpse into the financial world of their pastors and ministers.

So we move now to a point of curiosity of ministers and church people alike. What should we pay our pastor? How do we know if the amount is biblical and fair? What are some of the key issues we should consider?

To that "fun" topic we now turn.

Chapter 3

?$

The Minister's Salary: Is It Enough?

SO WHAT IS THE PRIMARY FINANCIAL ISSUE THESE MIN-
isters want to hear? If previous conversations are any
indication, the issue of ministers' salaries is one of the
hottest topics in the genre. Curiosity abounds, frustration multiplies, and communication breaks down.

Though no one can answer all of the questions on
ministers' salaries with precision, I hope the guidelines

and data in this chapter will be helpful. We'll look at a dozen or so of the more critical issues.

Salary Does Not Equal "Package"

The minister's financial package is one of the most misunderstood concepts in ministry finance. A package generally refers to all costs that a church pays for its minister. Those amounts would include salary, housing, health insurance, retirement benefits, travel and automobile expense reimbursements, and other expense reimbursements.

Let me share with you a real conversation. I have changed the names and rounded the numbers for simplicity. It took place on a church consultation of which I was a part.

"Dan" was a deacon in the church where "Frank" served as pastor. In our consultation interview with Dan, he expressed concern that Frank, the pastor, was overpaid. I asked him why.

"It's real clear to me. We are the same age. We have the same level of education. We have similar oversight responsibility if you look at the budgets we manage.

But the pastor makes $10,000 more than I do," Dan exclaimed. "He makes $70,000 and I make $60,000. Something's wrong here.

"Okay, " I said, "Let's look at the numbers. Your salary is $60,000, right?" Dan nodded affirmatively. "What does the company pay for your medical insurance? We need to add that to your salary," I said.

"You can't do that," Dan insisted. "That's not my salary.

"How much does your company pay toward your retirement?" I asked again.

Dan responded quickly, "What does that matter? That's not part of my salary."

"Okay," I continued. "Don't you have to fly every now and then for your job? That needs to be added, doesn't it?"

"Of course not," he began to say indignantly.

"You told me you just got back from a conference," I pressed. "Let's add that cost to your salary."

Dan looked at me with frustration. "What are you trying to prove?" he asked.

I began to write these numbers of paper.

- Pastor Frank's package: $70,000
- Retirement benefits: $5,000

- Conferences and convention reimbursements: $3,800
- Estimated automobile reimbursement: $5,200
- Health insurance: $6,000

"You've just said that retirement, conferences, travel, and health insurance should not be a part of your salary," I stated bluntly. "Okay, if you deduct those amounts from the total package the church is paying, Pastor Frank makes only $50,000. That's $10,000 below your pay."

"It looks like your pastor needs a raise," I concluded.

Some church members equate the dollars the church pays towards the cost of having a pastor to be the equivalent of the pastor's salary. That's not how it's done in the secular world. That's not how it should be calculated in the church world either.

Salary is not the same as package.

Most Ministers Are Underpaid

Anytime a discussion ensues about ministers' pay, someone wants to bring up the rare exception of a pastor being exorbitantly paid, or of the televangelist who made millions bilking people from his television studio perch.

Admittedly, there are occasional abuses of ministry pay. But let's not let the rare exceptions dominate the discussion when there is a greater need at stake. Most ministers are underpaid. Let's do the simple math.

For argument's sake, let's say there are 500 cases of year of overpaid ministers. I'm not convinced it's even close to that number, but let's use that as our number. There are approximately 1.2 million paid staff in Protestant churches in the United States. That means there are four cases of abuse for every 10,000 ministers. To look at it positively, there 9,996 underpaid or adequately paid ministers for every 10,000.

I understand that the number of exceptions should be zero. But it seems like a lot more effort is being put into the rare cases of indulgent ministers rather than the near epidemic of underpaid ministers.

Most Ministers Need a Raise and Would Like One

We did an informal survey of over 100 pastors. We simply asked them anonymously questions about their personal financial condition. Over 80 percent of them said they felt financial burdens. Many of them were using their credit cards to pay regular bills because they had no cash. Very few of them had any savings at all – not just contingency savings, but any savings.

The survey asked if they needed a raise. Most of them said yes. We then asked if they had broached the subject of a raise with anyone in the church. All of them, that's 100 percent, said no.

Ministers fear asking for raises for a number of reasons. First, they are aware that a few bad examples in ministry have poisoned perceptions for many. The abuses have gotten widespread publicity. A minister thinks that he will be associated with the bad guys if he even mentions the need.

He would rather get paid less, provide less for his family, than to be considered one who abuses his pastoral position.

Second, most ministers view money as an earthly issue. Their role is to focus on spiritual matters. They are to keep quiet, many presume, when any discussion of their pay takes place.

Third, there are always critics in the church looking for any issue to go after the pastor or other staff ministers. If a minister broaches the subject of a pay increase, he gives that critic ammunition to fire a barrage of verbal bullets. The pastor is keenly aware of such a risk; he, therefore, avoids any discussion of his pay.

Fourth, a pastor knows the hurts and needs of his members and those in the community. He is keenly aware that many are suffering worse than he is financially. He is very sensitive to speak about his own needs. When he has ministered to three families in the past year that declared bankruptcy, he feels terrible for even hinting that he and his family are struggling.

Fifth, we found that a number of church members think that any mention of financial needs by their pastor is a lack of faith. They freely quote out-of-context Bible verses to demonstrate the weak faith of the pastor who is courageous enough to mention his need.

Of course, most of the critics of a pastor's pay would gladly accept a raise in their own jobs. It's just different for their pastor, they surmise.

Most Ministers' Financial Burdens Exacerbate the Pressure They Are Already Feeling

Though I could give examples for any church ministry position, take for a moment the life of a pastor. In the course of a week, his life interacts with a myriad of scenarios.

He ministers to a dying person.

He does the funeral of a good friend.

He has to tell the couple in the church that their son was just killed in an auto accident.

He visits the cell of 44-year-old businessman sentenced to seven years for embezzlement.

He takes the call of a 35-year-old man who has just learned he has widespread cancer.

He counsels numerous people who have marriage problems, financial problems, health problems, emotional problems, and family problems. He is expected to be omnipresent, whether it's the local high school basketball game or the latest Sunday school class social.

He must deal with the business affairs of the church. He often supervises other ministers, many of whom look to him for guidance.

I could go on and on. Such is the life of a pastor. The pressure is enormous. The highs and lows are never-ending and yet unpredictable.

Why should this man come home to a wife who has been crying because they don't have the money to pay the bills? Why should the church let financial needs pile on to the enormous pressures he already has? Where does it say in the Bible that a pastor should never have enough income to send his kids to the state university?

Don't get me wrong. I fully understand that a pastor accepts the reality of the pressure and highs and lows when he obediently answers the call to ministry. My purpose is not to make you feel sorry for him. Rather, I encourage church leaders and members to do everything they can to help the pastor in his many challenges. And one of the greatest ways to help is to make certain your pastor has an adequate salary.

Some Pastors Leave Churches for Financial Reasons

I love Florida. I have lived in both St. Petersburg, Florida and Boca Raton, Florida. I love the tropical environment, the year-round sunshine, and the easy access to either the Atlantic Ocean or the Gulf of Mexico.

I lived in Boca Raton as an adult and St. Petersburg as a child. My dad was a pastor in St. Petersburg. He still recalls his years there as some of the best years of his life and ministry. And he really thought he would have a lifetime ministry there.

But he didn't. Instead he left after only three years.

I was hurt when we left St. Petersburg, but I did not know the full reason why until I was an adult. Dad admitted to my brothers and me that he thinks he made a mistake in leaving the church there. You see, he left because he could not support our family of five on his salary of $18,000. He did have medical insurance benefits and an automobile reimbursement up to $3,000. He had no retirement benefits.

The church had an attendance of 110 when he arrived, but it grew rapidly, consistently going over 300 and more. The budget tripled, but my father never got a raise.

And guess what? He never mentioned his struggles to anyone but my mom.

Though my two brothers and I were unaware at the time, times really got tough for my parents. The financial pressure was enormous. At times dad would have to swallow his pride and check food out of our own church's food pantry.

Dad finally left the church he loved. He has regrets to this day. He loved his staff, the location, and the life he lived – except for his financial plight. He left to go to a church where he could support his family financially.

A few members who were in the know later questioned him about leaving. He admitted that he left for financial reasons, and they were hurt that he didn't come to him with his need.

My dad now thinks he should have done just that.

But I wonder why the members didn't do something without his asking. His salary was printed each month on the church budget that all members received. They knew his income and they knew his family size. And a few members knew he was a recipient of the food ministry.

Too many ministers leave their churches for the sole reason of financial needs. And most of those ministers are simply too reticent to say anything to anyone about their needs.

Ministers Typically Lack Financial Acumen

My brothers and I are fortunate. Like our father, we all have finance degrees, and we all worked in the business world before we answered the call to vocational ministry. But most ministers have little or no training in business and financial matters. Many of them have Bible degrees from Christian and Bible colleges. Others may go to seminary to get graduate degrees, but rare is the seminary that offers any training in personal or organizational finance.

I have talked with countless ministers who not only lack the knowledge about ministry finance, budgets, mortgages, credit scores, and consumer loans, but they typically don't know where to turn to get the best advice and counsel.

Later in this book, I will be talking about building a trusted team for your financial matters. Also, I will address the often-complicated issue of retirement. In chapter 5, we will look at the very specialized ministry issues of housing and social security. Though this book is far from comprehensive, it is my goal to answer the questions I hear the most, and to point ministers to resources and people they can count on in the future.

The Issue of Other Ministry Income

There is no prescribed manual for all ministers on the right protocol for receiving other ministry income such as weddings, funerals, revivals, and conferences. Some denominations or judicatories have very specific guidelines. A few churches have their own guidelines as well. But most do not. That is why ministers frequently ask questions related to other ministry income.

First, let me say clearly that there is not just one way to deal with ministry income. In most cases, there is no right or wrong. What I have done is talked with dozens of ministers and devised "best practices." You certainly have much flexibility with these practices.

Second, all ministry income as taxable and should be reported, typically on Schedule C. Some ministers argue that it is gift income and is therefore exempt from taxation. The IRS is clear, however, that this income is earned in the course of your work and is thus subject to taxation.

Best Practice #1: It is okay to accept other ministry income.

You have earned this income by conducting a funeral, officiating a wedding, or speaking somewhere beyond your church. You had to prepare extra work. You sometimes had to give up your weekends, particularly with weddings. It is one extra assignment to a schedule that is already busy.

Best Practice #2: It is generally advisable not to set fees.

Leave the amount that you will receive to those you are serving. Sure, that means you will sometimes receive very little and other times receive nothing. But you are already receiving a salary from your church. Fee setting typically sends the wrong message.

Best Practice #3: Be willing to do these services for nothing.

There will be some situations where the family or organization has very little financial means. Accept the reality that a certain number of your weddings, funerals, and speaking engagements will result in no outside income. For example, civic organizations and schools rarely will pay someone to speak. And there will be times that it is obvious the family or person cannot pay. Graciously decline any offers they make, and be grateful for the opportunity to minister to them.

Best Practice #4: Always express gratitude for anything you receive.

I know a few pastors who take a few minutes to write a brief handwritten note every time the receive a honorarium or stipend. That is a class act that should be emulated by others.

Best Practice #5: Do not anticipate other ministry income in your budget.

Other ministry income is unpredictable, uneven, and usually modest in amount. Do not build your financial lifestyle predicting these funds. Decide ahead of time how that money will be used and stick to it. Some ministers put it toward retirement. Some put it toward special savings accounts for items like automobiles. Some put it aside for their children's college fund. Some use it to pay down extra principal on debt.

And some give the funds to their spouses for extra spending money.

A Word to Church Lay Leaders about Ministry Finance

I anticipate that some who bought this book are not pastors or ministers, but laypersons who desire to learn more about ministry finance. Perhaps you have a great love for your pastor, and you were curious to find out how you might help him in this area.

Please allow me to make a suggestion.

Find out the person in your church who has the greatest influence over financial matters dealing with your ministry staff. Many times that person is a good leader who seeks to balance the financial realities of the church with the needs of the minister. He or she is always on the watch to discern how the minister can best be helped.

But, sadly, there are times when that person sought the position because he wants to be in control. He may have little or no desire to do look after the financial interests of the minister. He rarely recommends raises.

He offers stingy benefits to the staff. He is testy about any expense submitted for reimbursement.

That type of person in the church will make life miserable for the minister. He certainly will not help him in any way financially. If you discover such a situation, you may, at some point, have the opportunity to offer a new person for the job. If not, you can become the advocate for the minister until someone else can take the position.

Most church members are not aware how the person who controls the personnel purse strings can impact the emotional and financial wellbeing of your minister. It's worth taking a look.

To Keep or Not to Keep the Minister's Salary Public?

There are certainly divided opinions about this issue. Stated simply, should the minister's salary be kept public before all church members on a regular basis? For example, some churches distribute the monthly budget receipts and expenses of the church. In that monthly report you often see, to the dollar, exactly how much each minister makes.

Other churches provide only a total of all personnel costs or salaries. An individual minister's salary is not visible in the total.

Some churches have policies or denominational guidelines about how this matter should be handled. But most don't. So, for the vast majority of churches that have no guidelines or guiding principles on this issue, what is the best direction to take?

First, it is not a moral issue of right or wrong as long as there are no deceptive practices taking place. Second, most people, not just ministers, are uncomfortable having their salaries displayed before the public on a regular basis. Some positions in the secular world require such disclosure as with politicians and executives in publicly traded companies. But most people do not have to deal with the prying eyes of personal finances.

Is there a way then to provide the best of both worlds? Allow the minister a modicum of privacy while maintaining a culture of openness in the church? In many churches, the minister's individual salary is not made available for general public consumption. Any member, however, has the right to come to the church office to see the salaries if he or she desires.

Most members really don't worry or think about such matters. But, for those who do, the information is readily available.

Every church will have its own personality and thus have its own way of approaching this tension between transparency and privacy. Some ministers have no problem with their salaries being visible to all; others will struggle. For the latter group, the suggestion above may have merit.

Don't Forget the Bivocational Heroes

As many as one-half of the churches in the United States have a pastor who is bivocational. He has to keep a job beyond the church because the church cannot afford to pay him a fulltime salary.

These ministers are my heroes.

There really is no such thing as a part-time church. The demands of ministry in the smallest of churches typically require a full-time commitment. In essence, these ministers are working two full-time jobs though the churches do not offer a full-time salary.

It is difficult to have specific guidelines for every bivocational church, because they all differ in size, demographics, and financial capability. However, allow me to offer these general guidelines for paying ministers of these churches.

1. *Be as generous as possible.*

Some churches seem to want to pay as little as they can. With these heroes, why not take an opposite approach? Pay as much as you can without hurting the financial health of the church. If you expect the minister to give you 20 hours a week, calculate what one-half of a fair salary would be. Counting sermon preparation time and basic ministerial duties, that is usually the minimum the minister will be working. If you can't pay him one-half of full-time salary, pay him as generously as the church is able.

2. *Review the arrangement at least annually.*

Many times a bivocational pastor gets an initial salary and then it's all but forgotten by the church. It is possible that, after a year or so, the church has adequate funds to increase the pay. At the very least a small increase may be in order as a token of thanks for his service. Don't forget him just because he has another job.

3. *Get creative.*

Find out the needs of your minister and see if there are members who might could meet those needs. Does he need work on his home? Could he use help with his yard? Does a member have a place on the lake he and his family could use for a week a year? Perhaps the church does not have the financial strength to pay him fulltime. There are still ways you can "pay" your minister with something other than money.

4. *Maximize his tax benefits.*

Most of his salary might be rightly classified as a housing allowance as allowed by the Internal Revenue Service. This is covered in Chapter 5. If so, the pay from the church would not be federally taxable and, usually, not state taxable as well. In other words, the partial income the church pays him could go a lot further.

How Much Should You Pay a Guest Preacher?

Eventually, your church will have a guest preacher. Your pastor may be out of town or he needs time to focus on other areas of the church. When this happens, you are faced with the question, "How much should we pay the guest preacher?"

Most of us want to show the guest preacher our appreciation through an honorarium. We desire for him to feel valued and loved but still be good stewards of the church budget. It is a tension many church administrators feel.

Here are four guidelines I suggest for navigating this tension:

1. *Cover travel.*

As soon as the visiting preacher steps into his car or boards a plane, he becomes your guest. Plan to cover the flight or car mileage. The IRS' current standard mileage rate is $0.56 per mile. I recommend reimbursing at that rate. Depending on the anticipated mileage, you may consider offering him a rental car.

2. *Cover food.*

Yes, he would be eating whether he was preaching at your church or staying at home. But he is your guest, and you are his host. A good host will take care of the food. If you are eating out with him, use your credit card. If he has a meal on his own, have him send the church the receipt and reimburse him.

3. *Cover accommodations.*

If the guest preacher has to stay overnight, pay for the accommodations. Having to stay overnight is not a perk for a guest pastor. It is a sacrifice he makes to speak at your church. Most would much rather be at home with their wife and kids. Be sure to cover any hotel costs.

4. *Base the honorarium off your pastor's salary (including housing allowance).*

This is where most struggle because of the number of variables involved – audience size, number of services, and expected length of teaching all play a role.

Here is my logic for basing the honorarium off your pastor's salary.

You have already decided to pay your pastor a certain amount based on his current responsibilities. Among these responsibilities are the variables at play with a guest preacher's honorarium. Your pastor is already responsible for speaking to a certain size audience for a certain length of time. Since these variables are already considered, use this salary as your starting point.

For every service, pay your guest preacher .5% of the pastor's salary.

Here's a quick example:

- Pastor's salary (includes housing allowance): $60,000

- Number of services: 2

- Guest pastor's honorarium: $60,000 x .5% = $300 x 2 services = $600

I would probably round up to the nearest $250. For this example, we would end up giving the guest pastor a $750 honorarium.

This method should allow you to be generous without compromising your stewardship.

For those with a part-time pastor or for those without a pastor, base the calculation on what you would pay a full-time pastor.

As with any of these methods, this one is sure to have its flaws. The type of speaking engagement needs consideration. A Wednesday luncheon is not the same as a Sunday morning service. Therefore, adjustments should be made accordingly. However, this method can provide you a way to be consistent and have the guest preacher leaving with a sense of your church's appreciation.

In Conclusion: What IS a Fair Salary for a Minister?

After all, that is the title of this book! As you might anticipate, there is no single answer. But many churches do overlook ways to evaluate the fairness of the minister's salary. Here are some guidelines and resources. I am not advocating you follow all of these guidelines, though you may. I do hope one or more are helpful to you and your church.

1.   *Denominational resources*

Many denominations have conducted extensive studies of ministers' salaries based upon a myriad of factors: Age, experience, education, size of church, position, and others. Though such a guideline may not be precise for your church, it certainly can be helpful.

2. Independent resources

There are numbers of studies and guidelines on ministers' salaries beyond denominational works. Rather than mentioning any one or more by name, I recommend you do a quick Internet search of "ministers salaries guidelines." You will receive a plethora of choices.

3. Look for the median

Imagine half of your congregation on one side of the worship center. They would represent the 50 percent that have the lower household incomes. Now put the second half on the other side of the worship center. They are the families in the upper 50 percent. Stand in the middle. Where do you guess the middle to be? What is that salary? Some advocate that such a place is a good salary for the pastor. Half of the families make more than he does; half the families make less.

4. *Education*

I am a firm believer that education should be a factor in ministers' salaries. It is expensive and hard work to get a bachelor's degree, a master's degree, and a doctoral degree. A bachelor's degree takes at least four years. The basic seminary master's degree, the master of divinity, is a three- to four-year degree. The Ph.D. from a seminary rarely gets done in less than four years. That adds up to about 12 years of college and graduate education. A medical doctor, by comparison, needs eight to nine years to get his undergraduate degree and medical degree, three to four years less than a minister with a doctoral degree.

The salary of a minister should reflect the years, expense, and hard work that went into the educational process. Unfortunately, many ministers carry student loans for years after they finish their formal education.

5. *Comparison with Similar Churches*

My guess is that every church member and every minister knows about a church similar to their own church. It may be a church in the same denomination. It may be a church of similar size. It may be a church in similar demographics. Find a trusted source in one or several of those churches. You are likely to get a good idea what the range should be for your minister.

6. *Above All: Be Prayerfully Fair*

I have seen too many churches try to pay their ministers as little as they can. They know the minister is in a difficult position to negotiate lest he appear to be money-driven. I strongly encourage churches to take a different approach.

Ask how we can honor our ministers by paying them a fair wage. Ask how we can take financial pressure off them since they deal day by day with so many other pressures. Ask the ministers themselves if they have financial needs.

I bet many of them will speak freely if only asked.

And as you are working toward a prayerful and fair salary for your pastor and other ministers, help him in his financial affairs in both the present and the future. Most ministers are woefully prepared for the day when they desire to retire or, for some other reason, are forced to retire.

Indeed retirement for the minister is a very big issue that many churches give little thought. We will address that issue in some detail in the next chapter.

Chapter 4

?
$

Your Retirement

WE'LL CALL HIM "DONALD," BUT HE COULD HAVE BEEN a number of people. Donald served faithfully as a pastor for 42 years in several churches. He and his wife Terri had great plans for retirement. Because of limited means, they had not traveled much. There was so much of the United States they wanted to see. They didn't dream of traveling internationally. They would be happy with domestic trips.

Donald and Terri had three children and five grandchildren. From their small town in Missouri, they looked forward to traveling to Atlanta, Minneapolis, and El Paso to visit the three families. Terri had her own "bucket" list of places she wanted to visit. As the final year of Donald's final pastorate approached, the couple began to take an assessment of their financial readiness for retirement. Their plan throughout their years had been basic:

> Make certain they or their church put a regular amount into the denominational retirement fund every paycheck.

> Put an additional amount in a savings account.

> Use the small retirement fund Terri had accumulated from working part time for several years.

> Sell their home and rent a small place. Take the equity from the sale and use those funds for retirement.

It sounds like a reasonable plan, doesn't it? Let's see how they fared.

The couple was astonished and dismayed to discover how little had been put in the denominational retirement account over the years. Two churches that represented fourteen years of Donald's pastorates put only one percent of his salary toward retirement.

Though they put funds in a savings account with the best of intentions to use them for retirement, it never worked out. They needed another car. A child needed help at college. Terri had some uncovered medical costs. The list could go on. The "retirement" savings fund was all but depleted.

Terri knew her part-time employer didn't put much into her retirement account, but she soon discovered the real meaning of "nominal."

When they approached a realtor friend about selling their home, they learned a new meaning for "upside down." The Great Recession had decimated the value of their home that they had purchased, unfortunately, at peak value. They were horrified to find out their home was worth less than the amount of the outstanding mortgage. They were "upside down."

Donald and Terri, like millions of other potential retirees, had to reevaluate retirement. Donald decided to transition to interim pastorates and supply preaching. Terri went back to work two days a week. Their retirement and big travel plans were postponed to later.

Or maybe never.

Why The Retirement Plight Seems Worse with Ministers

Ministers in particular seem to be in trouble at retirement age. Many are surprised at their predicaments. Some become bitter at what they perceive to be shoddy treatment by their former churches. Look at some of the reasons why. See if you identify with any of them.

Many ministers have no financial training. Their educational path may have included Bible college and/or seminary. It is rare to get any business training in those institutions. Some ministers even have an aversion to learning about finances.

Most churches don't have sophisticated benefits plans like corporations. They often put what they can toward the minister's retirement. Some put nothing toward retirement.

Some ministers have an attitude that God will provide regardless of their own stewardship. While that attitude has no biblical basis, it is still pervasive in some ministry circles.

Ministers are often reluctant to get a financial advisor to guide them through the morass of financial issues, and retirement is one of the more complicated.

As noted earlier in this book, many ministers are not paid adequately. They are unable to contribute to a retirement plan.

If you can relate to any one of these, I hope to provide you with some guidance to a solution.

Two Simple Rules

If I could get ministers to follow two simple rules, most of the retirement problems could be solved. Though it's simplistic, it's worth heeding.

Rule #1: Put something aside for retirement, even if it's a small amount, every paycheck.

Rule #2: Begin as early and young as possible.

Look at this simple example. If you could set aside $265 a month for every month beginning at age 25 until you retire at age 65, you would be a millionaire at retirement at an 8% rate of return. If you waited until you were 40 years old and you wanted to retire as a millionaire, you would need to set aside $1,650 a month instead of $265 a month. That is called the beauty of compound interest.

Those numbers may seem daunting. And that's okay. For now, set aside as much as you can for retirement. Or you may be in your 50s now and you think your situation is hopeless. It's not. Just get aggressive and set aside as much as you can. Forego pleasures of today for security for tomorrow.

Is There an Ideal Formula for Retirement?

The simple answer to that question is "no." There is, however, a guideline that a number of ministers have used with great success. Some call it the 10-10-10 rule; and others call it the 70-30 rule.

The first step is to determine that you will live off only 70% of your after-tax income. That may mean that you may have to downsize your home or make significant changes in your lifestyle. You then take the remaining 30% of your paycheck and put a minimum of 10% for your tithe, a minimum of 10% for retirement; and a minimum of 10% for shorter-term savings needs.

Every minister I know who has practiced this approach to giving and savings has reported great results.

You may not be able to move fully toward 70-30, but you can try a less aggressive approach. For example, you may need to start with the 80-20 guideline. Live off 80% of your after-tax income. Give 10% toward the tithe, and 5% each to retirement and shorter-term savings.

The key is to get started.

My Situation Is Bleak! What Do I Do?

A number of ministers laugh at me when we start talking about retirement. Some are over-committed in debt. Others saw the values of their homes hurt dramatically during the 2008 recession. Several years later, they continue to deal with the consequences. Their financial picture remains scarred. Still others barely make it from paycheck to paycheck. The thought of putting any aside for retirement seems laughable.

Unfortunately, I have heard from many ministers in such a bleak situation. If you are in a similar situation, I encourage you to read this book in its entirety. In the last chapter, I broach the subject of finding a trusted advisor who can walk with you in what may seem like a deep and dark valley. That advisor may even find ways you can put a small amount aside for retirement. He or she may be a member of your church, someone with influence who can get the church to do its duty to help you with retirement.

Please do not give up.

Your spouse, family, and church need you to keep going.

So Many Choices

I once met with a minister who was ready to get serious about retirement. He had just turned forty and had no money set aside for retirement. With a trusted advisor helping him in the church, he had a breakthrough. The church agreed to pay 50% for every dollar he contributed to retirement, up to a maximum of 5% of the minister's salary. In other words, if he contributed 10% toward retirement, the church would add another 5%.

He was excited, because he could really see the possibilities of seriously catching up with 15% contributed each year. The church left him, however, with the responsibility of finding the right retirement vehicle. He came to me, and I began to talk about Individual Retirement Accounts, qualified plans, unqualified plans, 403(b)s, 408(p)s, and others.

After a few moments, he wanted a break from the conversation. He was so confused by the possibilities and names that his head was splitting. I explained to him that, ideally, he should put his funds in a qualified plan, because his contribution is subtracted from taxable income, and thus that amount is tax sheltered. Ultimately, though, I stopped confusing him with the choices and sent him back to his trusted advisor. The church ultimately set him up on a 403(b) plan through the denomination. Thus, he was able to put significant funds aside for retirement and get those contributions sheltered from current income taxes.

The minister then found out that his task was not over. He had to pick a fund or funds within the 403(b) to invest his retirement. The 403(b) was simply the vehicle; it was not the fund itself. When he began to look at a dozen choices, he became confused again. I could see why. Here is a partial list of his choices:

Large blend.

Large growth.

Large value.

Mid-cap growth.

Mid-cap value.

Small blend.

Small growth.

Foreign large blend.

Real estate.

World allocation.

Moderate allocation.

Retirement income.

Intermediate-term bond.

Inflation-protected bond.

Stable value.

No wonder he came to me for advice. When I looked at the funds, I was relieved to find that his denomination's retirement choices included one of my favorites. They are generally called "target funds." You select the date you plan to retire; then pick a fund that has that retirement date. For example, his choice of funds included the following:

Target date 2010-2015.

Target date 2016-2025.

Target date 2026-2035.

Target date 2036-2045.

Target date 2046-2055.

My friend planned to retire somewhere around 2040, so he picked the fund "Target date 2036-2045." The fund managers will take care of all the investing from this point forward. As the minister gets closer to retirement, his fund becomes more conservative. His chances of losing money are less. While he is many years from retirement, however, the fund will take greater risks. When the fund loses money, it has many years to make up the losses and replace them with gains.

Please be cautious, however. There is no such thing as a risk-free fund. Target date funds manage your risk; they do not eliminate it. And not all target date funds are equal. Some are better managed than others. Some, even with the same dates, are riskier than others.

But if you decide on a target date fund, make the decision and walk away. Continue to contribute to it regularly, but don't agonize over it monthly or even yearly due to market fluctuations. Leave the managing to the fund manager. You trusted the fund in the beginning. Stick with it. Don't abandon it at the first market downturn. Months later, you will be glad you did not panic.

Retirement Is Near But I Can't Afford to Retire

It's a sad comment that I hear too frequently. The minister simply does not have the money necessary to retire. No matter how many ways it has been calculated, it just can't be done. What are the alternatives?

First, there are no magic bullets. You need to be prepared to make some tough decisions. Second, once you've made the decision, move forward. There is no need to kick yourself over previous bad judgments. There is no need to dwell in the land of "what if." There is no need to live a life of despondency and depression. Life is still a gift.

When someone approaches me with this situation, I ask a series of questions. Perhaps one or more will apply to you if you find yourself in this situation.

Have I missed something? Does my spouse have some retirement funds I missed? Does my spouse have social security income I have not counted?

Am I certain of the money I will need for my retirement lifestyle? Perhaps you overestimated the funds you will need for a comfortable retirement. Perhaps you will be okay with the amount you calculated.

Do I have any assets I can sell? Some retirees sell their homes and use the equity toward retirement. They typically move to smaller accommodations and rent. By the way, a reverse mortgage is a form of selling your home to get income. Though the television ads look great, make certain you get careful advice before you take that route. There are many cautions that need to be heeded.

Can I work a few more years? Maybe if you worked, say, three more years, you can delay your retirement and save aggressively. Many older baby boomers are taking this path. If you are eligible for Social Security income, delaying retirement will increase your monthly check. The increase applies all the way to age 70.

Can I find part-time income to supplement my retirement? Many ministers are in the fortunate position of being able to take interim positions or to supply preaching in churches. Not only does that keep the minister sharp in ministry, it provides supplemental income to his retirement.

Eight Retirement Steps to Take Now

Regardless of your age, you should evaluate your retirement status now. The younger you are, or the further you are from retirement, the more opportunities you have to make substantive changes. But, as I noted above, no situation should be regarded as hopeless.

1. *Find a trusted advisor.* I have already addressed this issue, and I will highlight its importance in the last chapter.

2. *Take an inventory of your current retirement funds.* How much do you have? Where is it invested? How much are you investing each month? Is your church contributing or matching your investment? Are you eligible for Social Security? Does your spouse have any retirement funds?

3. *Use a retirement calculator to determine where you are.* Your advisor can help here if you are uncertain about the questions. There are a few assumptions you will need to make. Retirement calculators are

available for free on the Internet. They can approach retirement from a number of angles. For example, let's say you are a minister who will not draw Social Security funds. You want to be able to retire in 20 years with today's equivalent of $40,000 a year. How much money will you need at retirement? If you assume that you will live 25 years past retirement, and that you can earn 6% on retirement funds, you will need $550,000 at retirement. Keep in mind that the retirement calculator assumes you will have no money left after 25 years if you enter that period. That means a 65-year-old would live to 90. If you think you'll live past 90, you will need even more funds at retirement. My favorite place for all financial calculators, including retirement calculators, is www.BankRate.com.

4. *Make decisions now about covering any shortfalls.* If you are not saving enough for retirement now, don't wait on making any decisions to cover the shortfall. You have

a number of options before you. You can determine that you can live on less once you retire. For example, in the scenario described in number three, you may decide you can live just fine on $35,000 a year in retirement. Or you can start making greater retirement contributions now. Or you can delay your retirement. The possibilities are many, but decisions need to be made sooner rather than later.

5. *Look at the possibility of supplementing income now.* I know one minister who, at age 48, discovered he had a retirement shortfall. He and his wife made the decision that 75% of all extra income would go toward retirement. So if he received funds for weddings, funerals, speaking engagements, and other sources, most of it went toward retirement. I think he will cover much of the gap this way.

6. *Prepare for worst-case scenarios the best you can.* Those scenarios include death, disability, and long-term care. Term life insurance is relatively inexpensive, de-

pending on your age and health. Disability insurance can be a bit costly. But long-term care is even more costly. Do what you can when you can to get some type of protection for those worst-case scenarios.

7. *Make any lifestyle changes to contribute more to retirement.* John and Patsy told me that they had zero funds to supplement retirement. They lived paycheck to paycheck. I looked at their expenditures and found out they were eating out an average of six times a month at an average cost of $32 per meal. While those expenditures aren't extravagant, they aren't necessary. They decided to eat only once a month and to put the difference toward retirement. They are each 36 years old, and have 30 more years before retirement. The five restaurant meals hey have given up provides an additional savings of $160 per month for retirement. If they can earn 6%, that decision alone will add over $160,000 to their retirement fund!

8. *Continue an annual check-up on your retirement.* Some financial advisors recommend you stay away from annual evaluations of your retirement. Though I disagree, I understand their sentiments. They don't want you looking at your total retirement funds after a bad year of investments. Indeed, there will be some up and down years. If you have a fund with a target date, it's really best that you stick with it. But you can make other adjustments if needed. It is for those reasons that I recommend you take these eight steps each year. With a good trusted advisor by your side, you can be certain you are on the right track to a healthy retirement.

Retirement planning is essential for the minister. It is one of the most critical facets of financial health you will have. But there are two other financial decisions that are unique to most ministers and not to the general public. Those are the minister's housing allowance and Social Security.

We'll look at those two "biggies" in the next chapter.

Chapter 5

Housing and Social Security

MINISTERS ARE TREATED DIFFERENTLY FOR TAX PUR-
poses more than most any other American citizens.

Ministers' tax treatments are unique. What does
that mean? On the one hand, it means that you have a
great opportunity to reduce your tax obligations legally

and ethically. On the other hand, if you don't follow all the rules in doing so, you could get in serious trouble.

There are two things I think I can say safely about you. First, you would be pleased to reduce your taxes legally and ethically. Second, you don't want to get in trouble with the Internal Revenue Service.

Your unique treatment as a minister revolves around two major issues: housing allowance and Social Security. They are very different in how the Internal Revenue Service views them, so we will take them one at time, beginning with housing.

Housing Allowance: Read Very Carefully!

There was a day many years ago when a minister was hypothetically confronted with one of two choices. He could accept the call to a church where the total salary was $40,000, or he could accept the call to a church where the salary was $30,000, but the church provided a parsonage with all utilities paid.

Now, work with me on these assumptions. Let's assume that he could discern that God was giving him an equal choice between the two churches. And let's assume that the two churches were equal in almost every way. The only difference was the way the churches paid.

The minister does a little homework. He finds out that the value of the second church providing a home comes to about $10,000 a year. So he has the choice of seemingly two equal pay situations. One church pays $40,000 a year, and the other church pays $30,000 a year but provides a home worth $10,000 a year.

We are going to make one final assumption. This choice takes place a few years before legislation was passed to allow ministers to have housing allowance.

Since all other factors are equal, which church does the pastor choose?

It's simple. He chooses the church with a $30,000 salary and parsonage worth about $10,000 a year.

Why?

If he chose the $40,000 salary, he would have to pay state and federal taxes on the entire amount. Putting aside such items as deductions and exemptions, if he paid 20% in taxes, he would owe $8,000 a year. But if he chose the $30,000 salary and $10,000 parsonage value, he would only be taxed on the $30,000 salary. Paying 20% tax on $30,000 comes to $6,000.

So he has to choose between paying $8,000 in taxes or $6,000 in taxes. It's a no-brainer.

The tax authorities and congress became aware of this inequity. In an attempt to solve the problem, laws were created that allowed pastors to exclude a portion of their salaries for housing, which in effect made that portion of their income tax free.

The key word there is *exclude*. The law did not merely allow a tax deduction, it allowed ministers to exclude a portion of their income. From an income tax perspective, it's as if the income never existed. It is a huge benefit for ministers.

Who Gets the Housing/Parsonage Allowance Exclusion?

Unfortunately, many ministers simply assume that they can take a housing allowance off their income. They don't read the very clear rules about becoming eligible. And many ministers, as a result, have had huge sums of back taxes, penalties, and interest.

I want you to have all the benefits the law allows on housing allowances. But I also want you to stay clearly within the boundaries of the law. Generally, there are three tests you must pass in order to be eligible for the housing allowance.

Test #1: You are employed by a church or an integral agency of a church. This one is pretty easy. If you are working for a legitimate church, you are fine. You pass the first test. It gets more complicated if you work for a Christian organization other than the church. Not all seminaries, schools, missions, or other religious organizations pass the test. Indeed the test is pretty arduous, but it is clear. If you work for a Christian organization other than a church, and you desire to get a housing allowance, your employer must meet eight criteria:

1. The organization was incorporated by a religious institution.

2. The name of the organization indicates a church relationship.

3. A religious organization continuously controls, manages, and maintains your organization.

4. Trustees or directors must be approved by a religious organization.

5. Trustees or directors may be removed by a religious organization.

6. Annual reports must be submitted to the religious organization.

7. The religious organization contributes to the support of your employer.

8. If your employers cease to exist, the assets would be turned over to a religious organization.

Test #2: You are performing ministerial services and help facilitate your church's worship. Those services include baptism, communion, weddings, funerals, preaching, Bible study, evangelism, music, administration of an eligible agency, and teaching or administrative duties in an eligible seminary or college. Basically, if you are in a church, you should be carrying out the normal duties of a minister and assisting in the worship of your church. If you are in the "integral agency" you must demonstrate that you are carrying out its normal religious duties.

Test #3: You are ordained or "the equivalent thereof." Ministers: hold on to your ordination certificates. That one piece of paper could determine if you are eligible for housing allowance or not. If you have been ordained to the ministry, and if you have the evidence to demonstrate it, you should have no problem with test 3. If, however, your church or religious body does not ordain, you must demonstrate that you perform similar functions as an ordained minister. Indeed, the wording of the law says that the *triggering event* is the assumption of the duties and functions of a minister.

How Much of a Minister's Salary Can Be Designated as Housing?

The question above is critical. In essence, it is asking how much of the minister's income can be excluded from income taxes. Frankly, this point is where more ministers get in trouble than any other place. Many designate too much and thus subject themselves to the risk of future audits, back taxes, penalties, and fines. But a number of ministers fail to take the housing allowance in an amount that is due them. As a result, they pay taxes they are not legally obliged to pay.

The amount of income a minister can designate as housing is subject to three tests. It is important for the minister to know that the legal housing limit is the **lowest** of the three amounts.

> *The amount actually spent to provide your home.*
>
> *The amount officially designated as a housing allowance by your employer.*
>
> *The fair rental value of the home, including furnishings, utilities, garage, etc.*

It's very important for you to understand each of these limits. Remember, your housing allowance cannot exceed the **lowest** of the three tests above.

The amount actually spent to provide for your home. It is critical that you keep good records of your housing expenses. I actually save all my bills and receipts, and print out all of my online bills that can be counted as housing. Make certain you include everything allowable by law. Here are some examples:

- Rent payments; mortgage payments; closing costs; down payments; etc.

- Real estate taxes.

- Insurance on your home and contents of your home.

- Improvements on your home; home repairs; upkeep of your home and contents. Consider such items as fence, pool, carpet, tiles, patio, appliance repair, garage, carport, room addition, invisible fence, security system and monthly fee, etc.

- Furnishings and appliances: vacuum; DVD player; television; piano; computer for personal use; washer; dryer; dishwasher; sewing machine, cookware; dishes; utensils; garage door opener; lawn mower; hedge trimmer; lawn blower; etc.

- Decorator items: drapes; rugs; pictures; decorative items; holiday decorative items; wallpaper; painting; sheets; towels; bedspreads, etc.

- Utilities: heat; electric; personal telephone; personal cell phone; water; sewer; garbage service; personal Internet; security system charges; cable television; etc.

- Miscellaneous: Anything that maintains the home, cleans the home, or supplies the home. Maid service or lawn care labor cannot be included.

The amount officially designated as a housing allowance by your employer. Your church or other religious employer must designate the amount of your housing allowance each year ahead of your payroll payments for the next year.

I always recommend to ministers to shoot a little high with this amount. For example, if your church designates $15,000 for your annual housing allowance, and your actual amount is $16,000, you can't go back and claim the extra $1,000. You are out for that year. But if your designated amount for that year was $17,000, you could claim the entire $16,000. You would then report on your tax statement $1,000 in income as "excess housing allowance."

The fair rental value of the home, including furnishings, utilities, garage, etc. This category is the most ambiguous of the three limitations. You first have to calculate what the annual rental value of your home without furnishings would be. If, for example, homes of similar size in your neighborhood rent for $1,500 per month, you could say the fair rental value of your home is $18,000 per year (1,500 x 12). Some accountants suggest that you multiply your home's market value by 1% to get the monthly rental value. So a home valued at $200,000 would have a monthly rental value of $2,000 (200,000 x .01). The annual rental value would thus be $24,000 (2,000 x 12).

But you must also add the value of utilities and the fair rental value of everything else in the home: furniture, garage, pictures, appliances, decorator items, etc. Those numbers are more subjective.

Important Takeaways on Housing Allowance

I've tried to keep this entire book on the minister's salary basic and clear. But I know, however, that these last few pages have been tedious. There have been a lot of numbers and some formulas that may not make sense. As I do throughout this book and, particularly, in the last chapter, I strongly recommend you get a trusted advisor to walk through these issues with you.

But there are some facts you need to know yourself about housing. Let me conclude this section with some of the most important facts for you to know.

A housing allowance is a huge tax benefit for ministers. It should not be ignored, and all the related laws should be followed carefully.

The Internal Revenue Service has clear guidelines that tells who is eligible for housing allowances. Follow those guidelines carefully and stay out of trouble.

An understated housing allowance results in lost tax benefits. An overstated housing allowance is not legal. You want to stay legal.

Mortgage interest can be a fascinating double benefit. The amount can be excluded from income in the housing allowance. That same amount can also be used as an itemized deduction.

Your housing allowance cannot exceed the minimum of three guidelines. Make certain you or your financial advisor understand these guidelines well.

Careful record keeping for your housing allowance is a must. You keep these records yourself in the event you are ever asked by the IRS to prove the amount of housing allowance you take each year.

The Social Security Enigma

There is much confusion about ministers and Social Security. Basically, some ministers pay into Social Security and some don't. There is a clear and important distinction between these two groups.

Those who pay into and are covered by Social Security essentially take no action. Unless a minister seeks to do otherwise, all ministers are covered by Social Security. The minister will make his quarterly payments as a self-employed person. Essentially that means that the church does not pay one-half of the amount as it does for other employees. So instead of paying the typical 7.65% of pretax income, a minister must pay double, 15.3% (these percentages include both Social Security and Medicare), since no employer is contributing to the amount.

The mystery of ministers and Social Security resides more in the second group, those who do not pay into the system. Among ministers, the more common question asked is, "Did you opt out of Social Security?"

Those who are considering opting out of Social Security must proceed carefully. I will highlight the main points you should consider.

The narrow window to opt out. Essentially a minister has two years after he has begun his ministry to make this decision. The Internal Revenue Service marks the timeline with the first two years a minister earns $400 or more in ministerial earnings. By the tax deadline (usually April 15) after the second year, a decision must be made. There is no appeal or backdating. If the minister misses this narrow window, he or she no longer has an opportunity to opt out of Social Security. By their inaction, ministers make a lifetime decision to pay into Social Security.

Only one way to opt out. There is only one place to receive exemption from Social Security payments: the Internal Revenue Service. Such exemptions cannot be granted by any other organizations or individuals. Also, there is only one form that is acceptable to apply for this exemption: Form 4361. With the narrow window of two years to apply for exemption, the minister must be very precise and careful if he or she decides to apply for exemption. Remember the 2-1-1 rule for Social Security exemption: 2 years to decide; 1 organization to seek exemption; 1 form to submit.

Only one reason to opt out. My father once told me that hundreds of ministers sought his advice on the decision to seek exemption from Social Security payments and coverage. In every case, he told the minister the same thing. The decision has to be yours and yours alone. It is not a matter of advice; it is a matter of conscience. Read very carefully the only reason to opt out: *Because of your religious principles, you are conscientiously opposed to accepting, for services performed as a member of the clergy, any public insurance, including Social Security.*

Your decision cannot be a mere financial decision. It is either based on the principles set forth by your denomination or your individual religious principles. If it is the latter, you should be able to discern what biblical principles were formative in your decision to opt out.

Allow me a moment to speak a word to anyone who advises ministers on this matter: don't! Whether you are another minister or a tax professional, the limit of your assistance should be to point the minister to the tax law, and to tell him or her that the decision is a matter of individual biblical conscience, not someone else's advice. It is likely a lifetime decision, so you don't want people having animosity toward you years later because they perceive you gave them poor guidance. Lead the individual to the law and let the matter be between him or her and God.

Assume your decision is a lifetime decision. The IRS law is clear that your decision to opt in or out of Social Security is an irrevocable lifetime decision. Indeed we see no indications that the law will change in the foreseeable future. Granted, there have been three occasions where Congress has opened a window for ministers to change their minds. A 1978 decision opened the window for ministers who were exempt to revoke their decisions. The window opened similarly in 1987 and 2001. The window has never opened for ministers who elected to stay in Social Security yet wanted to opt out later. It seems that the trend of Congress is that once you are in Social Security, you are there to stay. You should not count on any future moves by Congress, the courts, or the IRS to allow you to change your decision. Assume that your decision is indeed a lifetime decision.

Ministers Need Help

I never wrote this book with a sense that it would be the unabridged tome that would have every question answered for ministry finance. To the contrary, I kept the book brief because I did not want to address every nuance and facet of all the laws and financial implications for ministers.

Laws pertaining to ministry finance continue to evolve toward greater complexity. Those laws dealing with finance in general and personal finance in particular continue to move toward greater detail and frustrating complexity.

You probably did not need this book to encourage you to seek outside help. But when you read this chapter and the brief overview of housing and Social Security, you may have been convinced that you could not tackle all of your ministry finance matters alone.

More ministers have trouble with housing and Social Security matters than any other financial issues.

The purpose of this book has been to let you know about high level ministry finance issues, and then for you to work with others to make wise decisions. Every major issue of ministry finance has been covered. It is important that you have a conversational knowledge about these matters. If you don't, you could find yourself in a really difficult, stressful situation down the road.

You need to find someone who has your best interests at heart and who is well-versed in this often convoluted world of ministry finance. So the obvious questions follow. Where do I find such a person? What should his or her credentials look like? Can I really afford this advisor?

Those are all great questions. We will answer them in the next and final chapter.

Chapter 6

?

$

The Need for a Trusted Advisor

THERE MAY BE A FEW MINISTERS OUT THERE WHO HAVE all the evolving tax laws and code memorized. They may know the nuances of ministry finance to a fine science. But this is not the majority of ministers.

As much as anything you have read in this book, please read this part carefully. You need help with your finances.

Do not walk this journey alone.

Too much is at risk. And it's not just a financial risk. It's a time risk. It's a reputation risk. It's an emotional risk.

Find a trusted advisor to work with you on your personal finances. At the risk of redundancy, let's ask the question: Why do you need a trusted advisor? I can offer at least three key reasons.

Ministry Finance is Complicated

By this point you have read the challenges of personal finance in general and ministry personal finance in particular. The United States tax code is complicated. The issues related to ministers make it doubly complicated. Here are some of the questions every minister must answer:

Should I opt out of Social Security?

How do I pay my taxes as a self-employed person?

What can be counted legitimately as housing allowance?

What if I have more housing expenses than my declared allowance?

How do you account for automobile expenses?

What are the advantages and disadvantages of a parsonage over owing a home?

How do I account for non-ministry income?

I received a notice from the Internal Revenue Service that says I'm being audited. What do I do?

How do I report stipends from weddings, funerals, and other speaking engagements?

Should I prepare my tax returns myself?

What do I include on Schedule C?

How can my church arrange my financial package for best tax benefits?

It's tough to know all the laws related to taxes and ministry finance. And to make it more difficult, those laws are changing every year.

More Time for Ministry

I have never met a pastor or other ministers who have plenty of time on their hands. Balancing the needs of family and ministry is in itself a great challenge. Why would you want to spend the necessary time to keep up with all of the nuances of the tax code and then spend untold hours preparing your tax returns each year?

Usually the answer to that question is "cost."

It is indeed an expense to have a paid tax preparer. But I have found that most tax preparers will save us money that we would not have found on our own. And then there is the peace of mind that comes with knowing that a knowledgeable person has done all the work for us in preparing our tax returns.

My background and training is finance. But I can't keep up with all the tax laws and changes. I am not immersed in the tax code every day like financial professionals in the field. And, admittedly, I would rather be doing something else with my time.

My guess is that most of you have better things to do with your time. Get a trusted advisor. He or she will become an indispensible ally for you and your ministry.

You Are to Be "Above Reproach"

When the Apostle Paul gave Timothy the requirements for being an overseer (most churches today make that word equivalent to "pastor"), the first qualification he gave was to be "above reproach." The word "reproach" means disgrace, discredit, or blame-worthy. So a person who is above reproach is a person who has a solid, if not stellar, reputation in the community and beyond.

While there is no expectation of perfection, there is the biblical expectation that the minister, by the acceptance of the call, has placed himself in a position evaluated by very high standards. The qualification gets right to the heart of the minister's salary.

I wish you had the perspective I do to see how many ministers are hurting their ministries and even jeopardizing their jobs with financial behavior that is not above reproach. The minister is late paying his electric bill. The minister charges at the local grocery store but fails to pay in a timely manner. The IRS is auditing the minister because of the manner in which he handled his housing allowance.

The list could go on.

Frankly, a number of ministers just fail to see the connection between handling their finances and the qualifications for ministry. They are therefore caught off guard, perhaps even shocked, when they discover that their character has been called into question due to their financial mismanagement.

You really need at least two people to be above reproach in dealing with your personal finances. You are the first person. You cannot delegate character and the desire to do what is right.

But you also need a second person, a trusted advisor, to walk beside you. Even if you knew the tax code by memory, even if you were one of the sharpest financial minds in the world, you need someone else.

You need someone who can vouch for your integrity.

You need someone to lead you through the complicated morass of tax codes and ministry laws. You need someone who can speak for you and how you handle your finances.

You need a trusted advisor.

Now perhaps the first thought is the cost of a trusted advisor. It is indeed possible to pay somewhat high fees for such a person. And many of them are worth every penny. But it's also possible to find someone who will help you at no cost; they see their work as a ministry in your church.

My primary trusted advisor in finances has been my father. He has walked the road upon which I find myself. But I don't limit my influencers to him. There are many important people in my life who have helped me understand not only the world of personal finance, but also the very specific world of personal finance for ministers.

Ultimately, how you handle your finances will be determinative in how your character is assessed by others. It won't be the only factor; but it will be an important factor. And if you don't handle your finances well, soon your ministry will not be viewed as "above reproach." It is therefore vitally important to find that trusted advisor. Such a person or persons are out there for you. I hope I can guide you to find these people.

Finding a Trusted Advisor for Ministry Finance

Allow me to suggest three paths for you to take to make certain you are getting the best counsel regarding ministry finance. One of the paths is a book. The final two are people, though the final two could actually be one person.

As I have spoken to ministers and those who have advised ministers, I keep hearing of one publication that seems to rise above the noise of advice: *Worth's Income Tax Guide for Ministers*. I recently asked my father about the book, and he told me that he had purchased every edition since he became a pastor in 1984.

Worth's Income Tax Guide for Ministers has been published every year since 1973. It is the most dependable and factual resource in this genre of any I have seen. The author is Beverly J. Worth, one of the most successful authorities in the area of ministers' finance, particularly on those issues related to ministers' taxes. She also gets to practice what she writes since her husband is an ordained minister.

The book begins every year with changes and notable developments that could affect the ministers' taxes and finances. It is then filled with laws, forms, and advice unsurpassed by any other publication.

Does the book have a downside? For most ministers the material will be cumbersome and detailed. But I really don't know how they can present it otherwise. There is just so much information, and it has to be presented with precise wording. But even for those ministers who do not read the book in its entirety, it's a goldmine of information used as a reference guide.

Ministers also need a good professional tax preparer. When I say those words to a friend in the ministry, he or she inevitably expresses concern about the cost. I respond with three pieces of advice. First, ask for an estimate of the cost of preparing your annual tax return. The tax preparer will need some basic information from you. From that point the tax preparer should be able to give you a close estimate. The cost ultimately depends on how much time he or she spends on your return. And that time is usually related to how well you kept your records.

Second, I recommend you ask fellow ministers how much they pay for tax preparation. Ask someone specifically who seems to be in a similar ministry position as you and similar size church. If you ask five or six ministers, you will typically find their costs to be similar.

Third, I recommend you consider the cost of *not* having your taxes prepared professionally. One costly mistake or one audit is all you need to be convinced that you need someone to prepare your tax returns each year.

What are the qualifications of a good professional tax preparer? Some persons are more comfortable with those who have earned the C.P.A. credentials. Anyone who becomes a Certified Public Accountant has earned his or her credentials. That person has typically passed an arduous level of study of accounting in his or her college major. The CPA has also passed one of the most difficult aptitude tests in any field. And a CPA must do continuing study to maintain his or her credentials each year. Most CPAs are, without a doubt, competent in their field.

But there are thousands of tax preparers who are not CPAs. Among them are some highly qualified men and women who will do an outstanding job for you. You must simply ask several people, particularly ministers, to get good recommendations.

Perhaps the most overlooked characteristic of a professional tax preparer is his or her involvement working on ministry taxes. As you have seen throughout this book, ministry taxes are complicated and changing. You must have someone who has been doing dozens of ministry tax returns for years. The most impeccable of credentials cannot replace the experience of doing this specialized type of work. *Please hear this one issue clearly: find a tax preparer who has a wealth of experience doing ministers' taxes.*

In addition to recommending the book, *Worth's Income Tax Guide for Ministers*, and in addition to finding a professional tax preparer, I recommend you find someone who can provide you informal counsel about personal finance throughout the year.

Now it's very possible that the person who counsels you throughout the year is the same person who prepares your tax return. But it's more likely that it is a different person. You need someone that can work with you on everyday financial issues that don't ordinarily call for a CPA. For example, you may be getting ready to purchase an automobile, and you may need simple advice. How much cash should I put down? Can I really afford this car? Should I lease or borrow?

Though I'm not a professional tax preparer or a CPA, I do find myself offering ministers everyday financial advice. I'm careful not to get involved in areas beyond my expertise, but I am happy to help my fellow minister. I am certain there are tens of thousands of businessmen and businesswomen like me who would be happy to walk alongside minister.

Many of them will be thrilled you asked for their ongoing help. But they will not likely intrude unless you ask them.

Get a trusted advisor. Don't let pride stop you from asking for help. There are so many who are waiting for such an opportunity.

In Summary, In Essence: Your Sevenfold Checklist

As this book comes to a conclusion, I want to leave you with seven "musts." These are not merely summary items; they are pointers to the most critical issues in ministry finance.

Be a trusted advisor. If you've read this little book, you probably know more than 90 percent of all ministers. Point them to this book and other resources. Help others even as you are seeking help. If you are a layperson who has an interest in this topic, volunteer your counsel for other ministers. The worse thing that can happen is they tell you "no."

Evaluate your salary. You may not be able to do anything immediately, but you can find someone you trust to walk with you on this sensitive topic. Despite the publicity a few well-paid ministers make, I know many ministers are struggling quietly. They simply are not paid well.

Do not presume this book has all your financial answers; look to the other resources recommended. This book was kept simple and concise so it could be assimilated easily by most anyone. It is critical that you engage other people and other publications.

Find a comprehensive tax book. Again, I point you to both your tax preparer and *Worth's Income Tax Guide for Ministers.* At the risk of redundancy, I remind you that the tax code is complex, and that ministers' tax is even more complex. Get qualified and experienced help on taxes. You will not regret it.

Examine your housing allowance and social security status. Housing allowances and Social Security issues are the most troublesome and complex for most ministers. It is imperative you get sound advice in these areas. Not only are the subjects complex, failure to follow the IRS rules for either one can present the ministers with problems for years to come. Make certain you and a trusted advisor stay on top of these issues.

Find your trusted advisor. They are out there. They are willing to work alongside you as a ministry. Don't let pride stop you from asking for help.

Realize that the issue is more than money. I have spent much time talking about ministers' salaries and other financial issues. But I hope you have heard clearly that it's more than money. It's a matter of stewardship. It's a matter of your reputation. It's a matter of the health of your family and marriage. It's a matter of the effectiveness of your ministry.

Thank you for taking time read this concise book on your salary and other financial issues. I probably don't know you. And we may never meet this side of eternity. But please know that I have prayed for every person who has and will read this book. May you have a life and ministry that is above reproach. And may your financial stewardship, like all aspects of your ministry, be used in a great way for the glory of God.

Thank You

As always, I am thankful for my wife, Sarah. I am so grateful that I get to do life with you. You are a wonderful wife and mom.

Thank you to my two young sons, Nathaniel and Joshua. I love and am proud of you both. I am so glad that I get to be your dad.

Thank you to my dad, Thom Rainer. It is rare to have a dad, mentor, and friend wrapped into one person, but you did it.

Thank you to my mom, Nellie Jo. You are always encouraging and self-sacrificing.

Thank you to my two brothers, Sam and Jess. I love your families. I still can't believe that we created a publishing company together. Unreal.

And thank you to the people of Southeastern Baptist Theological Seminary. It is an honor to serve alongside every one of you.

Additional Resources
from Rainer Publishing

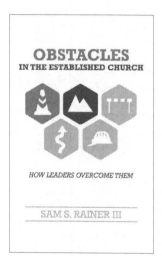

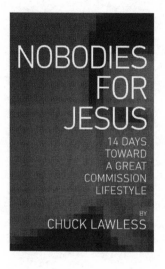

See more resources at

www.RainerPublishing.com

Made in the USA
Charleston, SC
12 May 2015